YOUR KNOWLEDGE HAS VALUE

Imprint:

Copyright © 2019 GRIN Verlag
Print and binding: Books on Demand GmbH, Norderstedt Germany
ISBN: 9783346002389

This book at GRIN:

https://www.grin.com/document/495189

Zain Mulk

A Comparison of the Atmospheric Pollution Between The Emirate of Dubai and Sharjah

GRIN Verlag

GRIN - Your knowledge has value

Since its foundation in 1998, GRIN has specialized in publishing academic texts by students, college teachers and other academics as e-book and printed book. The website www.grin.com is an ideal platform for presenting term papers, final papers, scientific essays, dissertations and specialist books.

Visit us on the internet:

http://www.grin.com/

http://www.facebook.com/grincom

http://www.twitter.com/grin_com

Table of Contents

Air Pollution within the UAE is a prevalent issue and has been for decades on end. The situation only seems to be getting worse, due to the collateral effects of urbanization. Dubai expects to host 25 million new visitors (John, 2019), thus the city looks to expand its urban sprawl, taking into account new construction projects, a greater population influx and higher numbers vehicular usage (motorisation). (Worldpopulationreview.com, 2017) reported that Dubai's population has been increasing at a rate of 10.3% as of late 2016, making it one of the world's fastest growing cities. Sharjah on the other hand, a city 30km away from Dubai, also seems to be expanding, through growing industrial activity and greater numbers of labour and working class residents settling in the Emirate. A high frequency of factories litter Sharjah's industrial areas, and densely packed traffic of heavy vehicles going to and coming from Dubai feed to the fumes released into the atmosphere. Moreover, both cities lie close to Dubai International Airport, one of the world's busiest and most crowded airports. It is evident that a myriad of factors come into play when determining the levels of air pollution between the two cities and it is crucial to compare the various effects and impacts of air pollution on the people of each city.

Aim

The goal of this report is:

- To determine which city is more polluted and to highlight the causes and effects of pollution on both cities. The decision will be made through 6 key factors: A general consensus, weather conditions and visibility, air pollution indices, traffic counts, city-specific lists and governmental data.
- To survey the impact of the effects on health on people of both cities.
- To gather and interpret primary and secondary data to determine and compare the scale and magnitude of air pollution on Dubai and Sharjah.
- To deduce the quality of air using the data gathered, thus making a final decision regarding the hypothesis.

Methodology

A questionnaire of 6 topically relevant inquiries are given to 25 residents of Dubai and 25 residents of Sharjah to determine the impact on health and the contribution residents of each city make to air pollution through their daily commutes around their respective cities. The importance behind the interviewees' answers are to:

1. Document whether the general public of each city take public transportation (e.g school bus, metro etc) or drive private vehicles as individuals on a day to day basis.
2. Record the average no. of people within each city suffering from breathing difficulties and at what frequencies do their difficulties occur.
3. Identify the proximity between surveyees homes and industrial activity
4. Record the frequency of travel journeys per day
5. Get an average of the number of cars owned (and in use) per person

- Two traffic counts will have been done on 1 suburban street per city for 10 minutes, once during the day and once at night, counting the total number of vehicles. The totals of each city will be compared with one another to determine which area has greater vehicular usage, thus inferring which city would likely have higher vehicular emissions.
- Furthermore, photographs of the cities' landscapes will be taken and its visibility, colour of sky and horizon will be analysed and compared with one another, as well as with a standard clean (clear) sky. All pictures will be of the same time on different days to insure that the same conditions are at play.
- Moreover, multiple air pollution indices for both cities will also be compared with one another and the different indices (from various sources) will also be compared for an accurate record of air quality for each city.
- Lastly, a list of pollutants emitted will be given in order to understand the effects and prominence of these on the two cities.

Area of Study

Area 1. Saheel Main Street, Arabian Ranches, Dubai

Traffic counts are done on two roads, one in Sharjah and one in Dubai. Dubai's area of study is a Suburban road, which lies on the way to a suburban community's shopping centre. The road is regarded as the community's main street, which connects to ongoing traffic on UAE's national highway E11.

This roadway is fairly clean and the abundance of trees, improves air quality on a regular basis, as CO2 emissions may be captured by surrounding vegetation. Loose sand and dust is not present, preventing any lifted dust, and a hazy roadway.

Area 2. Jamal Abdul Nasser Street, Majaz, Sharjah

This semi-suburban street is surrounded by residential apartments, away from the city's CBD, but is still a densely populated district. Sharjah's industrial area is 5 km west, which contributes to a polluted and hazy atmosphere to begin with.

Vehicular density is very high relative to streets in Dubai. Moreover, surrounding parking lots contain loose sand, allowing dust to lift up and create a hazy appearance. Trees are also lacking.

Data

Data 1.1: Questionnaire – Dubai residents

A questionnaire was carried out on 36 passer-by and online interviewees selected randomly. A large majority of the answers for Dubai had come from people in Dubai's busiest mall – The Dubai Mall.

Over a span of 2 hours, 11 recipients of the survey from Dubai and 3 recipients from Sharjah have had their answers recorded on an online Google form and on a sheet, in where each person's answers were tallied. The digital form kept a backup record for reference and for online surveyees.

Out of the 36, 20 spent most time in Dubai and 16 spent most time in Sharjah.

The initial question asked was, *'In which city do you spend most time in?'*, rather than 'in which city do you live in', to insure that the effects of the city in which most time is spent in was the city whose pollution effected the person, as time determines the accuracy of the effects rather than whether he/she resides in it or not.

Secondly, the survey asked, *'How often do you face breathing difficulties?'*, as. Breathing issues are a major effect of air pollution, and recording the % of people facing breathing difficulties in a specific city helps us understand the magnitude of pollution, as higher the % of victims of breathing difficulties, the greater the scale of air pollution, and its effect on the city.

Thirdly, the question *'How many vehicles do you own that are in use?'* determined the average number of cars per person on road. The higher the frequency of cars used, the higher each person's carbon footprint and the greater levels of emissions per person. If a majority use more than 2 cars, this can lead to excessive emission and dense roads.

Similar to the previous aim, the question *'How many journeys do you make per day?'* seeks to understand the frequency of car usage (how many times the vehicle is running and emitting)

4

and the density of vehicles on the road. The more journeys the more cars on road, some on the same road twice, thrice or more.

'How close is your home to an industrial area?', aims to find out the proximity of the average resident to a power plant or factory, which can tell us about the density of buildings and industries and how threatened the average resident is by nearby polluters.

Finally, the inquiry *into how one gets to work/school*, aims to record how many people use public transport and how many use private vehicles, which can determine, once again the carbon footprint per person and their role in the city's carbon emissions. The higher the % of people using private cars the higher the city's carbon footprint.

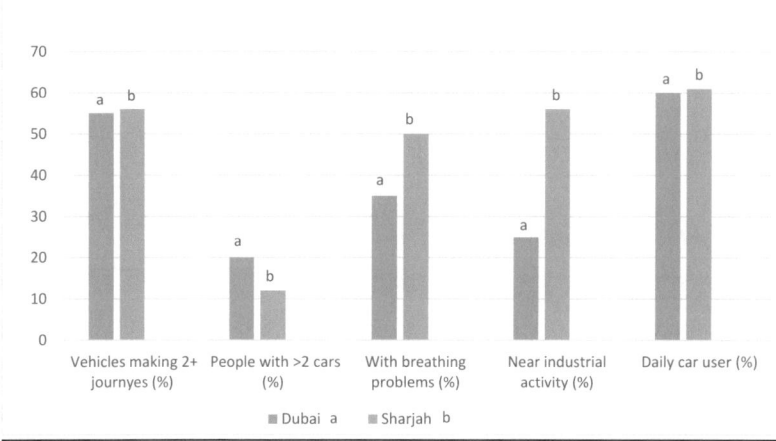

Results: The first two bars show a near equal result, where 55-57% of populations in both cities make more than two journeys.

The second bars show a low % of people in both cities with more than 2 cars, with an 8% difference when comparing the both. This may be due to the luxurious lifestyle in Dubai, where many own a myriad of possessions, vehicles being some of these possessions. Demographics show the average resident of Sharjah falling under a lower average income group compared to the average income group of someone in Dubai.

Thirdly, many more people in Sharjah face breathing difficulties than people in Dubai, as according to various maps of Sharjah, such as in Google maps, the industrial area covers a large portion of the city. Moreover, a lack of trees is evident in Sharjah, whereas in Dubai, trees sparsely scatter roads, communities and the CBD.

Fourthly, many more people in Sharjah live near industrial activity than people in Dubai due to the reason mentioned previously – industrial areas cover large parts of the city. This contributes to the amount of people in Sharjah facing breathing problems

Finally, the last two bars show that the no. of car users are nearly equal in both cities, as a majority of the population of U.A.E own their own cars.

Number of vehicles passing by an observing point (20 mins)
Location: Arabian Ranches, Main Street, (Suburban) Dubai
Date of Observation: 4/5/19   Observer: Zain Mulk
Duration: 10mins

Data 2.1 – Traffic count (Dubai)

Time Of Observation	Van	SUV/4X4/Crossover	Sedan	Heavy Vehicle	Minibus	Pickup	Other
10:00-10:10 PM	1	21	8	0	1	2	0
Total: 33							
6:20-6:30 PM	1	18	12	2	0	3	2
Total: 38							
Grand Total: 71	2	39	20	2	1	5	2

Data 2.2 – Traffic count (Sharjah)

Number of vehicles passing by an observing point (20 mins)							
Location: Majaz, (Semi Suburban), Sharjah							
Date of Observation: 11/5/19 Observer: Zain Mulk							
Time: 12:10-12:20pm and 6:20-6:30pm							
Duration: 10mins (x2)							
Time Of Observation	Van	SUV/4X4/Crossover	Sedan	Heavy Vehicle	Minibus	Pickup	Other
12:10-12:20 PM	0	34	52	0	0	12	1
Total: 99							
6:20-6:30 PM	1	30	47	0	0	4	0
Total: 82							
Grand Total: 181	1	64	99	0	0	16	1

Two random timings were selected for 2 counts per city, the first timing different for both cities, and the second the same, insuring one set of observation was in the morning and the other set at dusk (in the evening). Both cities were observed on the same day of the week – a Saturday.

For the first set of observations, the different times let me compare the traffic between two unbiased periods but in the morning of specifically a Saturday. Both first observations were followed by a second observation, this time both during 6:20-6:30pm on the same day of the week (Saturday). Similar to previous observations, both evening (6:00-6:15) counts had been 10 minutes long. The equal duration of the study insures unbiased conditions.

Results:

Firstly, the total number of cars passing by in the first observation in Dubai was 33, where a majority of the 33 were of SUV/4x4s at 63% (21/33 were 4 wheelers). The large minority seemed to be of Sedans at 24%, followed by the more polluting pickup trucks and a minibus.

The second Observation in Dubai seemed to repeat the first, establishing a consistent result. Once again SUV/4 wheels took a majority at 47%, followed by sedans at 32%

Comparing Dubai's count to Sharjah, seems to fit the hypothesis at a great extent when looking at the totals for both observations and consequently the grand totals of 181, compared to Dubai's 71. This is a difference of 110 vehicles in just a 10-minute gap and a difference of 155 %.

Other counts seem to fit the hypothesis in both observations (night and day). Sharjah had 25 more SUVs and 79 more Sedans, however, interestingly, Dubai and Sharjah had near equal no. of vans and bikes (other) with a difference of 1 each.

Interestingly, Dubai had 2 heavy vehicles and Sharjah none, and it is important to note that cities with higher air quality should have lower numbers of heavy vehicles polluting its roads. As mentioned by (ucsusa.org, 2018) 'Heavy-duty vehicles comprise only about 5 percent of all vehicles on the road, yet they generate more than 25 percent of global warming emissions that come from the transportation sector, and significant amounts of air pollution.'

Note: Sharjah's observation point (are of study) lay on a semi suburban area, generally busier than Dubai's quieter suburban area. This is because Sharjah's area of study is closer to the city centre and ironically Sharjah City Centre, compared to Dubai's area of study, which lies far from Dubai's city centre.

Data 3.1 – Visibility Photographs

The buildings at the skyline of Dubai and the camera are 15 km apart.

The Skyline of Sharjah and the camera are 6km apart.

Results:

The farthest buildings appear to be faint and blocked by what is likely dust. The same can be said for the skyline of Dubai, where Burj Khalifa's silhouette is seen but not the exterior.

However, taking distance into account, it is evident that Sharjah's visibility is poorer than Dubai's, as from a distance of 6km apart, the buildings appear faint and the horizon seems to be off white, indicating dust, whereas from a distance of 15km, although buildings cannot be seen better, the skyline of Dubai is very well noticeable and nearly as faint (fainter) as in Sharjah. Dubai's horizon also appears to be bluer (a deeper shade of blue) in colour than Sharjah's whitish blue.

8

Note: The photograph of Dubai has been taken in front of ongoing construction responsible for lifting dust, thus creating a hazier image than what should actually appear

Data 4.1: Air quality index

Air quality indices define the daily air quality of an area by the amounts of particles of pollutants per m3 and an 'overall' scale. In this report we will be comparing the Air quality index (using the US system) of Dubai and Sharjah over two days.

The sources this report will be getting its data from is 'Air-Quality.com', 'aqicn.com' and 'airvisual.com'.

Day 1: 12/5/19

Air-Quality.com

City	AQI	PM2.5	PM10	03	S02	CO	NO2
Dubai	164	81	154	113	11	236	20
Sharjah	173	98	142	146	13	240	19

Airvisual.com

Dubai: 156   Sharjah: 155

PM2.5 5.61 micrograms   PM: 7.69 micrograms

Data 4.2

Day 2: 13/5/19

Air-Quality.com

City	AQI	PM2.5	PM10	03	S02	CO	NO2
Dubai	154	62	121	110	3	158	2
Sharjah	158	70	121	142	5	184	4

Airvisual.com

Dubai: 140   Sharjah: 141

PM2.5 5.61 micrograms   PM: 7.69 micrograms

14/5/19

Aqicn.com

Dubai's Overall Index Reading: 151

Sharjah's Overall Index Reading: 151

Results: Both cities have equal overall readings, in two out of three sources. The first source seems to put Dubai's Air quality higher, using specific measures of individual pollutants. Since 2/3 were equal, the 3rd index (first in order) gives us the decider.

Listing the major pollutants:

- **PM2.5-** Particulate matter are tiny, fine particles suspended in the lower troposphere and consists of a mixture of solid and liquid particles able to enter small spaces, thus creating cardiovascular and respiratory illnesses, (Donaldson, K. and MacNee, W. (2019)). Their density allows them to remain low in the atmosphere and is responsible for creating a hazy appearing in the sky. As recorded by the index, Sharjah had higher levels of PM2.5 during both days. Once 98 and once 70 in Sharjah, the higher amounts are evident in the visibility photographs taken earlier, where Sharjah's horizon appeared hazier and off white closer to the surface, in contrast to Dubai's photographs, which had a bluer colour close to the surface
- PM10- The main difference between PM2.5 and PM10 is the size difference. PM10's diameter range is 10 micrometres to 2.5 and PM2.5's range is 2.5 or less. PM 10 has the potential to cause asthma, bronchitis, strokes and cardiovascular difficulties, according to Marlborough.govt.nz. (2019).
- Ozone – O3 in the troposphere can cause respiratory illnesses and can also reduce crop production and tree growth. It can also accumulate in smog which is detrimental to the human lungs, and can damage the protective linings in the lungs.
- SO2 – Sulphur Dioxide, is a pollutant released during industrial activity - when combusting fossil fuels, primarily coal in power plants. When cheap sulphurized coal is burnt, Sulphur can bond with 02 to form S02, which can escape out into the atmosphere through chimneys. The SO2 gas can then react with water vapour in clouds, creating and acidic precipitant, which can then come down as dilute sulphuric acid, thus creating acid rain.
- CO – Carbon Monoxide is an odourless, colourless and highly toxic gas, able to chock someone in minutes. When exposed to CO, the gas may get into one's blood stream, thus deoxygenating the blood and suffocating them due to the lack of oxygen.

The main cause CO emissions are vehicles. Heavy vehicles, emit large amounts of CO and vehicles without catalytic converters, cannot convert the CO into a nontoxic CO2, thus contributing to the CO concentrations. A basic solution for this may be, making catalytic converters, mandatory by law. CO is a prime issue in Dubai and Sharjah in every road where traffic density is high. The degree of CO in Dubai and Sharjah (especially the latter) is high, as many heavy vehicles have not installed Catalysts and cannot afford to do so as a catalytic converter is expensive due to its contents (heavy metals). In Sharjah, where income groups are generally low, a higher % do not have the filters installed, thus heightening the CO index on both days and every day.

- NO2- Polluters include: Vehicles and industrial activity. This gas can react with water vapour in clouds, forming nitric acid, thus acid rain and can cause respiratory illnesses. Levels are low, but can be lower, however, the burning of natural gas in the UAE contributes to the emissions

Conclusion

The hypothesis of this study, which states "Dubai's air quality is better than Sharjah's" is entirely right and justified by primary and secondary data that seems to support this.

Through the questionnaire answered by 36, people from Sharjah felt the worst of breathing difficulties, lived the closest to industrial activity, made slightly more numbers of journeys on average and had a higher % of car users (though nearly equal).

Sharjah had overwhelming numbers of cars in comparison to Dubai during both traffic counts, where all vehicle types besides motorbikes and heavy vehicles (by 1 and 2 more) were higher in Sharjah.

Although fainter in Dubai (due to distance), Sharjah's visibility and atmospheric conditions appeared worse side-by-side in comparison to Dubai, whose sky seemed clearer despite nearby construction.

Various indices, totalled out in favour of Dubai, and specific pollutants were more concentrated in Sharjah, thus all data checks out, establishing the hypothesis to be true

Finally, other surveys and report also compare Sharjah's air pollution to among the most polluted cities in the world. (The National, 2019) reported that the American University of Sharjah found Sharjah's air quality to be near equivalent to China's capital – Beijing and other cities, such as Mexico City and Tokyo, many of which are smog-ridden with high concentrations of VOCs, benzene and other toxic pollutants.

Therefore, through all data complied, compared and deduced, it is safe to establish that the hypothesis is indeed right and that Dubai's atmosphere as cleaner than Sharjah's.

Key note: It is important to note that the some of the primary data taken for this report was during the month of Ramadan, which may have altered the frequency of some cars, especially, during the evening observations, from 6:20-6:30pm as many in both cities break their fasts during that time period (6:55pm).

Weaknesses in this report

1. A lack of interviewees from Sharjah compared to the no. of interviewees from Dubai (16 to 20) means the %s for Sharjah were not as accurate as the % of Dubai.
2. An established list of the main vehicular polluters has not been included. It would have been ideal if the traffic count was supplemented by a list of the most polluting vehicles, in order of emissions. This would help us deduce and understand the traffic count better.
3. Finally, it would have been better if two roads of near equal crowd were compared with one another.

Strengths in this report

1. All data has been thoroughly interpreted and the reasons behind the results has been given. Data and statistics have been compared mathematically.
2. Primary data had given expected results that fit the hypothesis and predictions, and timings set for each observation were executed in the right time for equal conditions, when comparing the two cities.
3. A good average for Dubai was taken for the survey, of 20 people, from various age groups, races and gender, creating an accurate average. Moreover, both cities gave good amounts of data in the traffic.
4. Secondary data has also been compared using multiple sources to refer from a wide range references, once again increasing accuracy.

All in all, this report was able to meet its aims, however, some factors may have altered the result ever so slightly.

References and citations

1. John, I. (2019). *'Welcome the Future' campaign to woo 25m visitors to Expo 2020.* [online] Khaleej Times. Available at: https://www.khaleejtimes.com/welcome-the-future-campaign--to-woo-25m-visitors-to-expo-2020 [Accessed 15 May 2019].

2. Union of Concerned Scientists. (2019). *Cars, Trucks, Buses and Air Pollution.* [online] Available at: https://www.ucsusa.org/clean-vehicles/vehicles-air-pollution-and-human-health/cars-trucks-air-pollution [Accessed 15 May 2019].

3. Air-quality.com. (2019). *Sharjah Real-time Air Quality Index (AQI) & Pollution Report - Air Matters.* [online] Available at: https://air-quality.com/place/united-arab-emirates/sharjah/39b07414?lang=en&standard=aqi_us [Accessed 15 May 2019].

4. Airvisual.com. (2019). *Dubai Air Quality Index (AQI) and United Arab Emirates Air Pollution | AirVisual.* [online] Available at: https://www.airvisual.com/united-arab-emirates/dubai [Accessed 15 May 2019].

5. project, T. (2019). *Air Pollution in UAE: Real-time Air Quality Index Visual Map.* [online] aqicn.org. Available at: https://aqicn.org/map/uae/ [Accessed 15 May 2019].

6. Donaldson, K. and MacNee, W. (2019). *Potential mechanisms of adverse pulmonary and cardiovascular effects of particulate air pollution (PM10).*

7. Marlborough.govt.nz. (2019). *Health effects of PM10 - Marlborough District Council.* [online] Available at: https://www.marlborough.govt.nz/environment/air-quality/smoke-and-smog/health-effects-of-pm10 [Accessed 15 May 2019].

8. The National. (2019). *Air pollution in Sharjah as toxic as in Beijing, survey shows.* [online] Available at: https://www.thenational.ae/uae/environment/air-pollution-in-sharjah-as-toxic-as-in-beijing-survey-shows-1.270819 [Accessed 15 May 2019].

9. Moccae.gov.ae. (2019). *Air quality | Knowledge | UAE Ministry of Climate Change and Environment.* [online] Available at: https://www.moccae.gov.ae/en/knowledge-and-statistics/air-quality.aspx [Accessed 15 May 2019].

YOUR KNOWLEDGE HAS VALUE